BEVERLEY
THROUGH TIME
Patricia Deans
& Margeret Sumner

AMBERLEY PUBLISHING

Beverley, 1950s
This aerial view clearly demonstrates
Beverley's elongated town plan, running
along the line of the medieval 'high street',
or 'alta via', from the Minster to North Bar.
Wylies Road, Sow Hill and the bus station
were not built until the late 1960s. Until then
buses stopped (as here) at the southern end of
Saturday Market – except on Saturdays when
the market was held and they had to move
north beyond the Market Cross.

First published 2010

Amberley Publishing Plc
Cirencester Road, Chalford,
Stroud, Gloucestershire, GL6 8PE

www.amberley-books.com

Copyright © Patricia Deans
& Margeret Sumner, 2010

The right of Patricia Deans & Margeret Sumner
to be identified as the Authors of this work has
been asserted in accordance with the Copyrights,
Designs and Patents Act 1988.

ISBN 978 1 84868 624 3

British Library Cataloguing in Publication Data.

A catalogue record for this book is available from
the British Library.

Typeset in 9.5pt on 12pt Celeste.
Typesetting by Amberley Publishing.
Printed in the UK.

Introduction

Beverley is situated on the spring line at the foot of the Yorkshire Wolds, above the flood plain of the river Hull. Iron Age barrows discovered on Westwood show early settlers favoured the higher ground. But modern Beverley grew up around a monastery founded by John, successively bishop of Hexham and York, early in the eighth century.

By 1086 Beverley was a prosperous settlement. John's cult and shrine continued to grow in popularity as a centre of pilgrimage, particularly after his canonisation in 1037. And his monastery or mynster — a college of secular priests with substantial estates and privileges — served as a religious centre for the surrounding area. But the main source of Beverley's wealth lay in the wool trade, evidenced by modern street names like Walkergate, Dyer Lane and Flemingate. Local wool and cloth was exported via Beverley Beck and the River Hull, while the town's annual five-day fair attracted merchants from near and far — including the Low Countries. The original market area may well have encompassed Wednesday Market, Highgate and Eastgate. A second market place was later added to the north-west, while close by a chapel dedicated to St Mary served the growing population at that end of town.

The rights to the common pastures, which have helped to define Beverley's development, also date from this period. In 1258 the Archbishop of York permitted townsmen to pasture their animals on Westwood, Swinemoor and Figham in return for their agreement not to build upon these open spaces. All three remain common land; Westwood, in particular, has played a vital role in protecting Beverley from overbuilding and ensuring that the area west and north of the town centre remains its 'fairest part'.

In the eighteenth century the town became home to the Quarter Sessions and a popular social centre for local gentry families. The season revolved around the theatre, concerts, races and assemblies.

Notable public buildings such as the Guildhall, Market Cross and Assembly Rooms, were built, and Newbegin and North Bar became home to fashionable Georgian residences.

By the early nineteenth century Beverley had entered a period of decline. The town was little more than a local market centre, eclipsed in importance by Hull. But the coming of the railway in 1846 heralded a change in its fortunes. Tanning, shipbuilding, iron founding and light engineering all made their mark. Since their demise Beverley has become increasingly reliant on its role as an administrative centre for the wider area — as home to East Riding County Council (1889-1974), Humberside County Council (1974-1996), Beverley Borough Council (1974-1996) and currently East Riding of Yorkshire Council — and as an attractive place to live for commuters to Hull, York and Leeds.

But Beverley does not stand still. Modern developments over the last thirty years have seen the town expand rapidly, particularly to the north-east and south-west. Plans for the huge Hodgson's site, close to the Minster, have recently been approved. With a college, hotel, cinema, shops and housing, they imply a radical reorientation of the town.

North Bar Without, c. 1850

Medieval Beverley had no fortifications — simply a town ditch with several gates or 'bars' across the main roads. Eventually three substantial brick gates controlled access from the north and west — North Bar, Newbegin Bar (demolished 1790) and Keldgate Bar (demolished 1808). North Bar, the oldest surviving brick-built town gate in England, celebrated its 600th anniversary in 2009. Some 125,000 bricks were needed to build it – obtained from nineteen different local suppliers at a cost of roughly 3s 8d (18p) per 1,000.

North Bar Without, *c.* 1930

North Bar Chambers, Amphion House (No. 2 North Bar Without) and the first footpath under the bar were built in 1793-4 on the site of the early fifteenth-century St Mary's Hospital, which was by then in 'ruinous condition'. A century later the adjoining property was the house and shop of woodcarver James Elwell, who remodelled it on a lavish scale, with carved figures, heraldic shields and cartoon scenes featuring Disraeli and Gladstone. Far left stands Wylies House, demolished *c.* 1960 for the construction of Wylies Road.

North Bar/Bar House, c. 1865

The Bar displays the arms of Sir Michael Warton (*d*. 1688) — Beverley MP and owner of Bar House — topped by his crest, a squirrel. The house was remodelled in 1866 when the present balustrade and tower and a second footpath under the Bar were added. However, traces of the earlier house are still visible in the pillars of the garden wall. In the twentieth century Bar House was the home of Beverley artist Fred Elwell, son of James.

Rose and Crown, *c.* 1910

Originally the Bull, an inn has stood at this important junction just outside North Bar since at least the 1570s. In the mid-eighteenth century it played an important part in Beverley's early racing history. Landlord Robert Norris acted as clerk of the course, and owners came here to enter their horses in the races or stand them at stud. But in 1770 Norris moved to the nearby Blue Bell and took much of the race business with him. The pub acquired its present Tudor appearance in 1931 at the beginning of Fred Leach's long tenancy (1929-65). Only the tall middle block was incorporated into the new building, and the main entrance was moved from York Road to North Bar Without. Everything else was demolished, including two small shops which gave onto North Bar Without — occupied in 1899 by William Grantham, fruiterer, and John Dobson, butcher.

North Bar Within, *c.* 1920/*c.* 1970

North Bar Within was home to three eighteenth-century coaching inns — the Blue Bell, the Tiger and the King's Arms. The latter closed in 1926, but the bracket that supported the inn sign still remains. Next door is the Royal Standard, another pub with racing connections. Formerly the Turf Inn, its nineteenth-century landlords included Tom Green, the noted Beverley trainer. Mark Burgess first opened his famous ice-cream business here as a grocery in 1920, eventually occupying all three of the dormered cottages.

North Bar Within, 1897

Crowds return from sports held on Westwood as part of celebrations held for Queen Victoria's Diamond Jubilee, which also included balls, a procession to the Minster and a dinner for old people. On 23 July 2009 the street is crowded once again as townsfolk await the arrival of 1st Battalion, Yorkshire Regiment on its return from Kosovo and Iraq. Since Burgess' recent closure their premises have been redivided and the dormers restored — though not to match the originals.

North Bar, c. 1950

On 12 July 2009 the gates of North Bar were closed as it celebrated its 600th anniversary with a full day of events, including music from Beverley Brass Band and a medieval mystery play. Beverley had its own cycle of mystery plays, each performed by a different guild. The plays were staged on carts, which gathered at North Bar before setting off for the Beck, playing at six or seven different places en route. Before Wylies Road and Sow Hill were built in the 1960s, the Bar formed a considerable impediment to traffic. All vehicles coming from the north and west — including buses — had to pass through to reach the town centre. Here the traffic waiting at the Bar includes a cart — perhaps from Ireland's farm on Swinemoor Lane — still delivering milk in the churn.

North Bar, 1983/1996

North Bar only has 10 feet 9 inches (3.3 metres) of headroom – not enough for a standard double-decker. So in 1934 East Yorkshire Motor Services introduced a bus specially adapted for use on Beverley routes, with a top deck tapering inwards and a roof shaped to match the gateway. A broad white band was also painted around the front and sides of the roof to conceal its high crown. But large vehicles, including normal double-deckers, continued to get stuck. Damage was visible even in 1950, and by the mid-1990s the Bar was in urgent need of repair. Restoration work was completed in 1996 and the gates were rehung early on a Sunday morning. Modern traffic patterns now protect North Bar. But satellite navigation systems, misdirecting heavy goods vehicles, have recently posed an unexpected new threat.

Coronation Gardens, c. 1825

Nos. 55 and 57 North Bar Within (farthest right) form part of a grand terrace of five houses built in 1780. The house next door was demolished in 1827 to make way for St Mary's Cemetery. Only forty years later the cemetery was closed for new burials, and in 1955 it was refurbished as Beverley's Coronation Garden. Gravestones still line the walls, and the roofs of Armstrong's Garage — now St Mary's Court — are visible on the left.

North Bar Within, *c.* **1780**
The two gantries display bunches of grapes (the generic sign of an inn) and the signs of the Blue
Bell (now the Beverley Arms) and the Tiger. On the left is St Mary's Manor, rebuilt in 1803, later
home to the Ministry of Agriculture, and now converted into flats. The smaller properties next to
St Mary's church were demolished in the 1820s to improve the prospect of the house, ironically
now hidden from view by a wall and trees.

Tiger Inn, *c*. 1835

An important coaching inn between 1730 and 1847, the Tiger attracted a number of important visitors. Thomas Boswell certainly enjoyed his stay in May 1778, 'Good inn. Supped very heartily.' But on the death of landlord Samuel Greenwood the Tiger was sold to meet debts. The coaching trade had declined with the arrival of the railway, and competition from the Beverley Arms and Kings Arms was too fierce. The inn was subsequently divided into (and remains today) five separate shops.

Tiger Lane, *c.* **1880/c. 1960**
The Tiger Inn stood at the corner of Tiger Lane — previously Cuckstool Lane, the lane that led to the ducking stool. John Ellis Hopper, plumber and ironmonger, occupies one of the shops created from the inn. Opposite is a fifteenth-century building whose timber frame is hidden under plaster. In 1907 Gordon Armstrong opened his garage here, building cars and aeroplanes in the workshops to the rear. It now forms part of St Mary's Court, a shopping arcade opened in 1983.

North Bar Within, *c.* 1910

By 1910 another sign of the motoring age has appeared — the Beverley Arms no longer advertises stables but a garage! Quick & Clarke, estate agents, now occupy Grindell House (1740), designed by William Wrightson, builder of the contemporary Newbegin Bar House. Next door, Pizza Express serves diners in a building designed in 1861 as two semi-detached houses by Hull-born Cuthbert Brodrick, architect of Leeds Town Hall. Before the First World War it was the Beverley Club and more recently the Water Board offices.

North Bar Within, *c.* 1945

Buses passing through the Bar once stopped in front of St Mary's Manor. The pump still stands hereabouts — though not quite in its original position. By the late nineteenth century Beverley had at least forty public pumps. But the water they provided was often poor in quality and, despite vociferous opposition, a waterworks was built in 1881, near Broadgate Hospital. July 2009 presents a much more crowded scene as the Yorkshire Regiment parades past St Mary's.

Beverley Arms Hotel, *c. 1900/c. 1967*
Originally the Blue Bell, the Beverley Arms was rebuilt and renamed in 1794-6. Bought in 1852 by David Morley, landlord of the King's Head, it remained in the Morley family until 1920. The adjoining shop — latterly Arthur Jebson's butcher's — was demolished in 1967 when the hotel was extended. The premises of brushmaker John Westerby and saddler A. P. Clegg later became one shop. The building was occupied for many years by the Sheepskin Shoppe and is now a Chinese restaurant.

Wood Lane, 1886
This narrow entry leads into Wood Lane — a road of ancient origin first recorded in 1416 — which from 1861 to 1939 led to the Union Workhouse (now Westwood Hospital). The shops on either side were occupied by Smithson & Son, saddler, and Henry Sugdon, grocer. The shop next right was rebuilt in 1886 by William Hawe, designer of many Victorian villas and commercial buildings in Beverley, Driffield and Market Weighton. In the 1890s it was occupied by George Dales, draper.

Kemp's Corner, c. 1950

The junction of Lairgate and Saturday Market is still known as Kemp's Corner after John Kemp — printer, newsagent, bookseller, stationer and proprietor of the *Beverley Express* (1856-9). Kemp once occupied this prominent building, demolished in 1955 for road widening. Its slimmer replacement housed the Leeds Permanent Building Society until the Leeds merged with the Halifax in 1995 and is now Andrew & Rogers, optometrists. In 1950 Lairgate was still a two-way street and buses wait at the top of Saturday Market.

North Bar Within, 1860

The hanging sign (centre left) advertises the eighteenth-century Wheatsheaf, later the George and since *c.* 1900 the Beaver. Like many Beverley pubs, the Beaver was 'Tudorised' in the 1930s and looks very different today. The single-dormered Beverley Bank (right) opened in 1793 as Appleton, Machell & Smith. It later became the York Union Bank and was taken over by Barclays in the 1930s. The original building was demolished along with its neighbour in 1861 and replaced by the current Barclays Bank.

North Bar Within, 1977/1890s

North Bar Within is decorated for Queen Elizabeth II's Silver Jubilee. The green-painted premises of Fields (now a clothes shop) span the decades. This had been a chemist's shop since *c.* 1830 and Fields since *c.* 1889. Hawley's Antiques (nearest left) continues here today and was once William Whiting's grocery. Beyond Fields is Sonley's fishmonger's (now also a clothes shop)— run in 1899 by Thomas Trowill, dealer in game, poultry and fish.

St Mary's, Exterior, Pre-1850
While the Minster was the church of the archbishop, St Mary's was the church of the town and the guilds. The tower was rebuilt following the collapse of its medieval predecessor, with great loss of life, during a service in April 1520. Fortunately, many townsfolk were elsewhere — at a bear baiting — and an even greater disaster was averted. The flying buttresses were added during Victorian restorations by architects Augustus and Edward Pugin.

St Mary's, Interior

The oak pews were added when the sixteenth-century nave was refitted by George Gilbert Scott in 1864-7. The pilgrim rabbit, with his satchel and staff, appears (opposite a sheep's head) on the mouldings around the sacristy door. This jaunty figure has long been associated with the White Rabbit in Lewis Carroll's *Alice in Wonderland* — either as the inspiration for the character itself (Carroll's maternal grandfather, Charles Lutwidge, was Collector of Customs in Hull in the 1820s) or simply for Sir John Tenniel's famous illustrations.

Hengate, *c. 1920*

Known as Nellie's after its last landlady, the timber-framed White Horse was run by members of the Collinson family from 1892 until 1976, when it was sold to Samuel Smith's. The brewery installed a bar but otherwise left the nineteenth-century, gas-lit interior untouched. The buildings left of the mullion-windowed shop (now a barber's) were demolished when the bus station was built and the Manor Road/Norwood junction widened in 1968. Modern traffic patterns put a great deal of pressure on Hengate and its buildings.

Norwood, c. 1890
Old Porch House was demolished in the mid-1940s. The site was later occupied by the Clock Garage and is now home to Kwikfit. The adjoining cottage (left), with its late Georgian shop front, is now Beverley Music Centre. However, the buildings further left have disappeared, replaced by Majestic Wine Warehouse and Netto. The butcher's shop (far right) was also demolished and a modern replacement built. Once Thomas Musgrave (c. 1899-1937), then Healey and Son (1937-2008), it is now J. H. Family Butchers.

Beverley, Aerial View, *c.* 1980

Clearly visible (top right) are the bus station on Sow Hill Road, New Walkergate (under construction) and the cattle market. Livestock markets were once integral to Beverley's prosperity. They date back at least to the eighteenth century and were held quarterly on Norwood until 1865 when the cattle market was built. From the late nineteenth century the markets became more frequent — fortnightly from 1889, weekly from 1944, and twice weekly from 1954. A separate market for pigs was held behind the Globe Inn until 1895 when it too moved to the cattle market. The cattle market was closed and replaced by Tesco in 2002. Only a plaque on the supermarket wall remains to commemorate this important part of Beverley's agricultural past.

Walkergate/Norwood, c. 1900

The cottages behind the cyclist were demolished to provide access to Walkergate School (1906), replaced a century later by a residential home. In the background are the Beverley and East Riding Public Rooms, converted in 1935 into the Regal Cinema. John Carr's original assembly rooms (1761-2), which fronted onto Norwood, were demolished. But the large hall at the rear, added 1840-2, was retained. The Regal was demolished in 1999 and replaced by Regal Court, a modern development of shops and apartments.

Ladygate, April 1980

Nos. 35-37 Ladygate was a timber-framed house with a massive central chimney-stack. One of Beverley's earliest buildings, it later became Dale's Fish and Chip Saloon. Although listed in 1980, it was demolished soon after and replaced by the dormered modern buildings on the left — now an amusement arcade. The neighbouring Dog and Duck was built by John Smith's in 1929, replacing an older inn on the site. Opposite are the former Public Baths. Part of the late Victorian Corn Exchange development, they opened on the site of the eighteenth-century fish shambles in 1887 and closed in 1973. In 1976 Sellitt & Soon transferred their Beverley showroom here from its original site next door to the King's Head. The whole Corn Exchange complex was sold for redevelopment in 2006 (Sellitt's moving to Walkergate) and reopened as a department store, Browns of York, in March 2010.

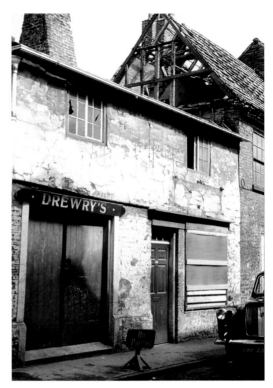

Ladygate, 1930s

In the nineteenth century brewing and beer dominated this end of Ladygate. No. 6 (now Mirchi Indian Restaurant) was the Ladygate Brewery and No. 7 (Ladygate Interiors), the maltings. Simson's photographer's (Ladygate Tandoori) was the brewery tap — the Custom House Vaults — with dram shop at the front and tap room behind. Other pubs included the Globe, the Lion and Lamb at No. 11 (Legends Clothing) and the Freemason's Arms at No. 3 (part of a private house).

Globe Inn, 1967

The seventeenth-century Globe Inn is soon to be demolished to make way for Sow Hill Road. A glazed door from the pub is preserved in the kitchen of a house in Keldgate, and the modern Globe Court, at the junction of Sow Hill and Ladygate, commemorates its name. The café was demolished along with the Globe, and the refurbished property is now William Brown, estate agents. Next door to tobacconist Frank Meadows (now Fawcett & Abraham) was Laughton's (later Pethick's) butcher's (now the Yorkshire Building Society). Buses briefly used Sow Hill Road to reach the stops in Saturday Market before the new bus station was built.

Ladygate, Aerial View, *c.* 1900

For centuries Ladygate enclosed the Sow Hill end of Saturday Market. The Globe Inn is visible here (bottom centre). The adjoining twin-dormered house was also demolished 1967-8. Now a café, the site remained vacant until the bus station was redeveloped *c.* 1983. Also prominent is Walkergate House (*c.* 1775), once the home of shipowner Henry Samman and now the East Riding Registry Office. And beside Toll Gavel Methodist church is the chimney of the Golden Ball Brewery on Walkergate.

Saturday Market, Aerial View, *c. 1960/c. 1980*
Saturday Market before and after the opening of Sow Hill Road. To the south the market is in full swing and the buses have gone from their normal stops to stand beyond the Market Cross. By 1980 the Golden Ball chimney has disappeared (the brewery was demolished in 1969). Instead, the County Hall extension (1931-2) stands out on the skyline. Originally two stories, but later doubled to four, it has now disappeared behind new buildings commissioned by Humberside County Council, 1981-6.

Saturday Market, c. 1910

A Saturday market has certainly been held in Beverley since 1293. And the market place — perhaps then extending as far as Hengate and Ladygate — may have been laid out a century earlier. The Edwardian market is much smaller than its modern equivalent. Opposite Butterdings, where stalls crowd together today, carriers' carts stand ready for loading and unloading. Meanwhile, a charabanc passes by, full of men smartly dressed in mufflers — perhaps on their way to the races?

Saturday Market, *c.* 1860

The Market Cross (a fine centrepiece for today's Christmas illuminations) dates from 1711-14. The board (far left) advertises the extensive range of teas offered by George Hobson, grocer. The adjoining shop was rebuilt *c.* 1863 by William Hawe, and Hobson traded here on the corner of Old Waste until *c.* 1906. Since then it has been a bank – first Midland, now HSBC. And at No. 1 Saturday Market the name of Beilby's saddler's lives on – clearly visible on the wall of the modern estate agency.

Butterdings, c. 1905

Certain areas of Saturday Market were devoted to particular goods, among them Sow Hill, Butter Dings and Corn Hill. Butterdings had been the site of the medieval archbishop's hall — a stone building known as the Dings. Akrill's gunmakers occupies one of a row of shops built in the 1750s. It opened in 1833 and remained in family ownership until it closed in 2001. A succession of cafés have recently occupied the premises, but the winged-wheel CTC (Cyclists' Touring Club) emblem still retains its place above the door.

Butterdings, c. 1882

The chimney of Ladygate Brewery dominates the scene. Guest & Philips Jewellers has traded here since 1966. Until 1924 their shop was the White Swan Hotel – in the 1890s scene of 'Variety Concerts Every Evening'. It still has a swan (replaced in 1978) above the door. The Push Inn was once occupied by James Mowld Robinson, apothecary and wine and spirit merchant. Robinson was six times mayor between 1842 and 1870, and also owned a brewery in Butcher Row, opposite the Angel.

Saturday Market, 1955/1988

The Market Cross has often been the focus of Beverley's celebrations. Here, for the first time, the Rotary Club has put up a Christmas tree in Saturday Market, and carols are sung around the Market Cross to raise funds for displaced children. Three decades later, L. C. Byass & Son's Burrell Showman's Engine and 87-key Gavioli Organ enliven a damp winter's afternoon. In the background are the ornate premises of the NatWest, built in 1864 for the Yorkshire Banking Company.

Saturday Market, *c.* 1895

Burton's Boot & Shoe Warehouse was originally part of a longer row of small shops
— perhaps of sixteenth-century origin. For many years a fruit shop below and a barber's
upstairs, it eventually fell into considerable disrepair, so exposing the original brick and
lath construction. Modernised and refurbished in 1996, it is now Viyella. The ornate
premises next door were originally built in 1853 for Charles Hobson, chemist. By the 1890s
the shop was occupied by Mrs Richardson, baker and confectioner. It was later home to
Rambla Bakeries and is now Multiyork. Immediately right is the shop of William Ramshaw,
watchmaker (now Beverley Building Society), and far right is Briggs & Powell Passage.

Corn Exchange, c. 1965/c. 1880

The original corn exchange was created in 1825 from part of the butchers' shambles (1753). It was demolished and a new exchange built on the same site in 1886. In 1911 Ernest Symmons opened Beverley's first cinema here — the Picture Playhouse — using his own generator since mains electricity only arrived in the town in 1930. By 1963 bingo had taken over. However, the Picture Playhouse — by then Beverley's only cinema — did reopen in 1982, finally closing in 2003.

Saturday Market, 1920s/*c.* 1956

In the 1920s carriers still stand opposite Butterdings, while florists J. Sellers & Son of Lairgate run their market stall. By the 1950s the scene has changed. The carts have gone, replaced by cars and buses at their temporary Saturday stops. But Beverley's nurserymen are still represented — now by Braithwaite's Queen's Toll Nurseries, Beckside. Dean Martin and Jerry Lewis appear in their last film together, *Hollywood or Bust*. And a Burgess' ice-cream van is there to provide a treat for weary shoppers and their children.

Saturday Market, 1955

The buses are back at their usual stops. The Yorkshire Bank (until 1959 the Yorkshire Penny Bank) has been here since *c.* 1925. However, the original mid-Georgian houses were demolished in the 1970s and replaced by a near-replica. And in July 2009 crowds await the start of cycling's National Elite Circuit Race Championship, returning to Beverley in 2010 for the third successive year. Events like this — including Literature, Food, Early Music and Folk Festivals — make a significant contribution to the local economy.

Saturday Market, *c.* 1960

Vera Holtby's petfood shop occupied the tall building at the corner of Ladygate — home a century earlier to corn factor William Westerby — while distinctive cream Hull Corporation callboxes can be seen in the middle of Corn Hill. Harry Robinson's butcher's shop (*c.* 1937-73) briefly provided premises for Sellitt & Soon but in 1976 became part of the King's Head. Now an optician's, the house next door was until 1925 another of Beverley's many inns — the Pack Horse.

Toll Gavel, 1974

Before pedestrianisation Toll Gavel was the main road to Hull and Hessle — clearly shown by the names painted on the road. Grocers Baggs & Son had traded in Beverley since before the First World War, first further down Toll Gavel and from *c.* 1920 at this site. Their shop closed in the early 1980s and is now Smiths Books. Moving left came Bonner's wallpaper shop and Selles chemist. Across the street, Burtons moved into its distinctive new building in 1937.

Toll Gavel, 1977

Decorations for the Queen's Silver Jubilee extended throughout the town centre. Shoppers crowd the narrow pavements and spill out into the road — a scene common before pedestrianisation in 1983. The black sign of Schofield's (now Evans/New Look) is visible (left). TV rental shops such as Rediffusion (right) and Granada, and small local supermarket chains like Goodfellows were typical of the '70s scene. Similar supermarkets on Toll Gavel alone included Baggs, Jacksons, Peter Debb and Frank Dee.

Toll Gavel, *c.* 1912
A branch of the Maypole Dairy Company once stood on the corner of Toll Gavel and Landress Lane. Founded in Wolverhampton in 1887, the Maypole chain grew rapidly. It traded mainly in butter, margarine, eggs, tea and condensed milk — much of it imported from Denmark. By 1915 there were 985 Maypole stores, including the Beverley branch, which opened here between 1905 and 1913. In the late 1940s men's outfitter Noel White & Bellamy moved in. The business stayed here after the site was redeveloped but eventually left in 1990 for Landress Lane. The shop is now a Julian Graves wholefoods store.

Toll Gavel, _c._ 1910

The hanging sign of the Golden Ball (front right) marks the prominent Beverley pub and brewery, run by the Stephenson family until its sale to Hull Brewery in 1919. On the left are the three gables of another pub — the Litchfield Hotel. Formerly known as the Red Lion, it was bought and renamed in the 1890s by prominent Beverley publican Robert Attwood Litchfield. The Litchfield closed in 1972 and is now the Halifax.

Toll Gavel/Cross Street, c. 1910

Baggs' grocery (now the British Heart Foundation) is seen here before its move further up Toll Gavel. A later long-time occupant was men's outfitter Ringrose. Two doors down are the premises (now part of Currys) of Francis Hall — bookseller, printer and proprietor of the *Beverley Independent*. Founded in 1888, the weekly *Independent* merged with the *Beverley Recorder* in 1911. Currys — then a gramophone/wireless dealer — first came to Beverley *c.* 1933, trading originally from No. 47 (now Clarks Shoes).

Cross Street/Toll Gavel, Early 1950s

The Keep Left sign shows traffic in Toll Gavel is still two-way. The Golden Ball closed in 1924 and Woolworths traded here from *c.* 1930 until January 2009. In July 2009 the store reopened as Boots. On the left is the Coop (now Wilkos). Beverley's Cooperative Society first opened at Nos. 25-31 Eastgate before the First World War — with other shops following in Toll Gavel, Wednesday Market and Grovehill Road. It merged with the larger Hull society in 1929 and opened here shortly afterwards.

Toll Gavel/Cross Street, 1981

The pedestrianisation of Toll Gavel and Butcher Row has reached this corner, but the old Hull/Hessle road sign is still in place. Stead & Simpson had traded on this site since the 1880s. When they left for new premises over the road, neighbouring Skeltons moved in — extending their shop and opening a café upstairs. But shop and café both closed in 2007 when Cooplands took over the Hull-based bakery chain.

Cross Street, Late 1970s

Ironmongers Pottage Brothers had operated in Cross Street since the 1920s. Woodhouse's furniture store is now Currys, while Le Gourmet has become Sullivan's Fish and Chips. East Riding Council's Customer Services Centre was formerly St Mary's National School (1849), popularly called the 'Square' School. It replaced an earlier school on this site and was supported by subscriptions, donations, school pence and charity income. In 1913 the school moved to Mill Lane and the building seen here later became part of County Hall.

Proclamation of King George V, Register Square, 11 May 1910

Richard Care, Mayor of Beverley, reads from the steps of the Guildhall, home of Beverley Corporation since 1501. He is surrounded by local dignitaries and musicians from the East Yorkshire Regiment and the Green Howards. Elected only two days earlier — his predecessor William H. Elwell had died in office on 23 April — Care was the first mayor in England sworn in under George V. The Post Office was built in 1905 when it moved from the corner of Cross Street.

Champney Road, 1992

The Temperance Hall was built in 1845 for £300 by the town's newly established Total Abstinence Society. The society was particularly well supported by the Primitive Methodists, among them the editor of the *Beverley Guardian*, assuring it of considerable press support. The new Magistrates Court was opened on the site in 2002 by the Lord Chancellor, Lord Irvine. The Treasure House extension to Beverley Library opened in January 2007, combining archive, museum, art gallery and local studies services.

Lower Toll Gavel, *c.* 1900

Hanging lamps mark the shop of Uriah Butters, draper and enthusiastic local photographer. The house of Anne Routh, a notable benefactor of the town, is now a café. Its red-framed display boards are set in recessed panels which mark window openings blocked to save window tax. Bon Marché — in the 1970s Frank Dee's supermarket — is on the site of the old Oddfellows Hall. The Independent Order of Oddfellows was a friendly society with a number of lodges in nineteenth-century Beverley.

Walkergate, 24 July 1912

A cart makes its way through flash floods caused when the culverted Walker Beck — which ran along Walkergate — overflowed after a cloudburst. On the corner is the shop of James Horner, tobacconist and dealer in glass and china. This was for many years Lightowler's painters and decorators, and is now a branch of Boots. Next door was the yard of George Pape, plumber, joiner and glazier. Then came the premises of William Dixon, Complete House Furnisher & Cycle Agent.

Butcher Row, *c.* 1905

William Dixon's business was flourishing. In 1899 he was trading at No. 5 (now Body Shop). By 1905 he had acquired the shop next door (Woodhead Bakers), and by 1912 he had added hairdresser David Robson's, marked here by the striped pole (Country Butchers). Next door to the Angel is Charles Mitchell, tobacconist and sports goods dealer. Across the street is the elaborately painted shop of Robert Campey, decorator. Established in Beverley since 1834, Campey's had recently moved from Well Lane.

Marble Arch

Known to some Beverlonians as the 'Marble Itch', the Marble Arch took its name from a local landmark — a passage that ran between the cottages and shops on Butcher Row demolished to make way for the cinema. Until trading ceased in 1947, the rival Picture Playhouse operated in a working corn exchange and cinemagoers sometimes found themselves picking grain off their seats! In contrast, the Marble Arch was a purpose-built cinema. Opened in 1916, under the management of Edward Butt, it could seat 1,100 people and also boasted a café. But by 1961 the Marble Arch, like its competitors, had turned to bingo, and the last film was shown in 1964. It finally closed in 1967 to be demolished and replaced by a supermarket.

Butcher Row, 1937

At the Marble Arch, Spencer Tracy and Franchot Tone star in *They Gave Him a Gun*. Next door, Gresswell & Co. was one of Beverley's larger shops, beginning life as a watchmaker's in 1914 before taking over the adjoining premises in the 1920s. All the properties featured here were demolished at the same time as the cinema. Only the small shop at the far edge of the picture survives. Later the Yorkshire Electricity Board showroom, it is now the Scope charity shop.

Butcher Row, Early 1980s

Various supermarket chains have occupied the Marble Arch site since the late 1960s — including Presto, Safeway, Somerfield and Marks & Spencer. Presto operated mainly in Scotland and northern England, opening its first store in Prestonpans (hence the name) in 1977. Opposite are a number of long-standing family businesses, all now gone: J. C. Peck, fish and chips (founded in 1915, now an amusement arcade); Harold Robinson, butcher (founded 1945, Lakeland); and, furthest right, the Beverley Bookshop (Millets).

Wednesday Market, c. 1870

Wednesday Market — once the medieval fish market — fell into disuse during the eighteenth century and remained a market in name only until stalls were reintroduced in 1984. The obelisk was built in 1762-3 to replace a market cross erected earlier in the century and was removed in 1881. At the top of Highgate, the façade of William Walls' butcher's shop (*c.* 1920) — until recently Larard's estate agency — has just been uncovered.

Wednesday Market, 1991

Highgate House lost its two southerly bays in 1909 to make way for Lord Roberts Road. Later the Gas Board showroom, it is now occupied by Lockings Solicitors. The Primitive Methodist chapel (see opposite) closed in 1955, to be replaced first by Crystal Garage and in 1994 by the present Boyes store. Primitive Methodism had arrived in the East Riding in 1819. The first chapel on this site (built 1825) was demolished in 1867-8 to make way for this enormous building, capable of holding 700 worshippers. Next door, Ye Olde Porke Shoppe is still in business. From 1845 to 1937 it doubled as a beerhouse — the Spotted Cow — run *c.* 1900 by Benjamin Ramshaw, pork butcher and beer retailer, and latterly by George Rawson. West End House (see opposite) was a draper's. Later the premises of D. H. Witty, printer and stationer, it too was demolished for the garage.

Wednesday Market, *c.* 1921

Jack's delicatessen and Peck's fishmonger's are two long-established family businesses, both with origins in Eastgate. George Jack ran the Eastgate Market (formerly Care's) before his son David began trading in Wednesday Market in 1960, while Harold Peck moved here in 1938. The Queen's Head certainly dates back until 1802 and may be the sixteenth-century Hart. Its original red brick had been rendered in 1899 and it was Tudorised by Darley's Brewery in 1926. Next door, Robson's hairdressing saloon had moved from Butcher Row *c.* 1905.

Wilbert Lane, c. 1900

Dating back to the 1860s, the Moulders Arms commemorates the industrial past of this area. Warehouses (rear right) mark the site of the original Crosskill Ironworks, founded c. 1827 by the son of a Beverley whitesmith. By the 1850s over 800 men were employed in works extending on both sides of Wilbert Lane. The original business was sold in 1864 (eventually closing in 1879), but that same year Crosskill's sons set up a new enterprise — William Crosskill & Sons — in Eastgate.

Beverley Station, *c.* **1970**

The railway came to Beverley in 1846 when George Hudson's York and North Midland Railway opened its Hull to Bridlington line. A line to York followed in 1865 but closed a century later. G. T. Andrews' station building underwent some changes over the years. A canopy was added over the entrance, and under British Railways orange North Eastern Region signs appeared. In 1993 the station was restored to something like its original appearance. The two wings now house Cerutti's restaurant and delicatessen.

Beverley Station, July 1988/*c.*1960

Steam traction ended on the Beverley line in the 1960s but specials still came through. *Mallard*, a class A4 Pacific, remains the holder of the speed record for steam locomotives – 125.88 mph (202.58 km/h), achieved south of Grantham on 3 July 1938. Here enthusiasts flock to see the newly-restored loco and celebrate the fiftieth anniversary of its record-breaking run. Meanwhile, back in the days of steam, Standard Class 3 2-6-0 locomotive No. 77012 from York pulls into Beverley hauling the Directors' Coach.

Beverley Station, c. 1965

Like many British Railways stations, Beverley had a small garden assiduously cultivated by its staff. The gardens — which lay between the station and the signal box — are long gone. But they have been replaced to some extent by the floral displays which have brightened Station Square since it was paved (and given a clock) in 1990. And both provide a link with the horticultural past of this area — in the 1820s the site of William Tindall's nursery gardens.

Beverley Beck, *c.* 1900

The Beck has linked Beverley to the Humber and the sea since medieval times. The canal fell into decline when modern barges grew too big to enter the waterway, and commercial use ended in 1987. In recent years the council has invested about £3 million in restoring and dredging the Beck, and it is now home to a number of leisure craft, as well as the historic barge *Syntan*, formerly owned and operated by Hodgson's Tannery.

Beverley Beck, *c.* **1900**
Humber keels gather alongside Barker's Linseed Mill. The Beck is slightly wider here so vessels could turn. The single-masted, square-rigged keels were the workhorse of the Humber basin for over 500 years. Seed crushing produced linseed oil, used to make putty by mixing it with whiting — crushed chalk — from Westwood. Later Barker and Lee Smith, the mill was converted to animal feed production in 1952 and demolished *c.* 2000 for the Barker's Wharf housing development.

River Hull, 15 April 1969

Now an industrial site, Beverley shipyard operated from 1882 to 1977. It was run by several different companies — most prominently Cook, Welton & Gemmell (1901-63) — and in 1969 by C. D. Holmes Ltd. The wet-fish stern trawler *C. S. Forester* — seen here — was the last trawler launched in Beverley. Built for Newington Trawlers of Hull, the ship was fired on by an Icelandic gunboat during the Cod War in 1973 and eventually passed into Icelandic ownership as the *Solbakur*.

Flemingate, 1952

Lightning F2s of 92 Squadron take part in a farewell fly-past before leaving RAF Leconfield for Germany; since then Air Sea Rescue helicopters have maintained a lone RAF presence on the former bomber base. Behind the Minster is Armstrong's Patents, and far right Hodgson's Tannery. Several tanneries once operated on the southern edge of Beverley, and Hodgson's (founded in 1812) came to predominate. On its closure in 1978, part of the site became a chemical works, while part was reused for the Museum of Army Transport. In 2009 everything has gone — cleared for a major redevelopment scheme.

Sun Inn, c. 1920

Dating back to the sixteenth century, and then called the Tabard, this ancient, timber-framed inn is reputedly the oldest pub in the East Riding. It has been known as the Sun since at least 1794 and was originally three separate dwellings. In 1872 landlord George Wiles was fined for keeping a disorderly house and left soon after. In 1994 it was renamed the Tap and Spile in an unpopular pub branding exercise but reverted to its historic name in 2000.

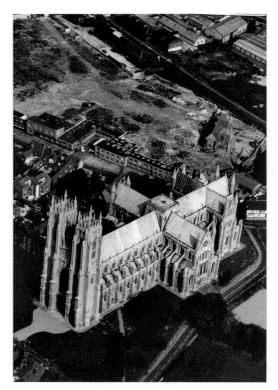

Beverley Minster/Eastgate, 1981
The ground uncovered by the Lurk Lane dig (front centre) was later developed for housing. The dig (1979-82) uncovered evidence of two successive pre-Conquest monasteries. Behind the Minster, Armstrong Patents — once one of Beverley's major employers — is being demolished. In 1914 Gordon Armstrong converted his works in North Bar Within to the production of 4.5 inch Howitzer shells and later bought Crosskill's old Eastgate site to increase output. Armstrong moved his main works here in 1919, returning to the manufacture of car components, including his own patented shock-absorber. The site is now the Cloisters, a mixed development of houses, flats and sheltered accommodation.

Beverley Friary, *c.* 1970

Armstrong's factory developed around Beverley's thirteenth-century Dominican Friary, a rare survivor among medieval friary buildings. By 1960 the friary — long subdivided into three separate dwellings — was in a poor state of repair. But Armstrong's decision to purchase and demolish the building triggered a prolonged campaign to save it. Restoration work was completed in 1974 and ten years later the friary opened as a youth hostel. The present building is just a fragment of a much larger complex. Most of the church, for example, now lies under the railway line.

Eastgate, c. 1900

The Victorian extension to the Minster vicarage (near left) was demolished along with the three adjoining cottages for road widening in the early 1960s. Grocer Richard Care (opposite) seems to have the decorators in — perhaps from his neighbours Moody & Sons (the last dormered house on the left). Care — three times mayor of Beverley — also had a larger shop in Saturday Market. Hidden by the bend in the road is the Eastgate site of William Crosskill & Sons.

Beverley Minster/Hall Garth, *c.* 1900

The archbishops left the Dings in the thirteenth century — transferring ownership to the town — and moved to the moated Hall Garth site, south of the Minster. By the 1820s some of the surviving buildings had become the Hall Garth Inn (or Admiral Duncan). But having a pub this close to his church so upset long-serving vicar Canon Nolloth that, in 1896, he bought it and closed it down. The Hall Garth became a farmhouse and was eventually demolished in 1958.

Highgate, *c.* 1920

Also known as Londoners' Street after the London merchants attending the annual Cross fair, Highgate was originally part of the 'high street' running from the Minster to North Bar. In July 2009 the Mayor of Beverley, Councillor David Elvidge, sets off along that route as part of the Bar 600 celebrations – behind him the Church Lads' and Girls' Brigade band and children from local primary schools. They will soon pass the old George and Dragon (more recently the Monk's Walk). A pub since at least 1802, its Georgian exterior hides a medieval hall. Two doors down is a house which once belonged to Colonel Oliver de Lancey, member of a powerful New York family and a loyalist during the American War of Independence. He died in Beverley in 1785 and is buried in the Minster. Delancey Street, the main thoroughfare of Manhattan's Lower East Side, commemorates the family.

Highgate, *c. 1977/1900*

Highgate is seen here decorated for another celebration — the Queen's Silver Jubilee. The Minster, however, is part-covered by scaffolding. Unusually for an Anglican church, responsibility for its repair and maintenance lies not with the Parochial Church Council but with the Beverley Minster Old Fund, a charity established in 1579. In 1974 the Fund Trustees decided that the Minster urgently needed a comprehensive programme of repair and restoration. £500,000 was raised in less than two years, and between 1976 and 1984 the Minster was scarcely ever free of scaffolding. The Minster yard was originally surrounded by a wall but this was dismantled and replaced by iron railings in 1905. On the left, a red-brick terrace (see opposite) has replaced characteristic single-storey Beverley cottages with dormer windows and sliding sashes.

Beverley Minster, 2002

The magnificent nave of Beverley Minster is seen here decorated for the Queen's Golden Jubilee service. The Minster was rebuilt after the collapse of the central tower *c.* 1213, and the fourteenth-century nave blends harmoniously with the earlier east end and crossing. The original trussed-rafter roof of the nave survives. Oaks from Bishop Burton and elsewhere were given in 1388, and an indulgence to fund 'new work' promoted in 1408.

Beverley Minster, c. 1975
A treadwheel — operated here by
architectural historian Ivan Hall — is
situated in the roof of the Minster above
the central crossing. The wheel raises a
decorative boss in the vault, so creating an
opening which allows building materials to
be winched up into the roof space. It was
installed in the early eighteenth century to
facilitate a major restoration programme,
overseen by Nicholas Hawksmoor and
undertaken by William Thornton of York,
which did much to protect the fabric of the
church. The Minster now offers a regular
programme of roof tours to its visitors.

Anne Routh's Hospital, Keldgate, 1884

In 1722 Anne Routh bequeathed the income from her Yorkshire estates to provide accommodation and a small weekly allowance for up to six poor widows. The will remained mired in Chancery until 1740, but almshouses with accommodation for twelve widows were eventually built in 1749, and rooms for eight more were added in 1788. The hospital was enlarged again in 1810 when a new building for twelve was erected next door in the same distinctive style as James Moyser's original.

Old Grammar School/Beverley Grammar School

Originally attached to the Minster, Beverley Grammar School is one of the oldest schools in England. In 1816-17 it moved from the churchyard to a new site adjoining the master's house in Keldgate (the present Old Grammar School). The school itself was closed in 1878 and later demolished. Refounded in 1890 on Albert Terrace, the school moved to its present Queensgate site in 1902. The sports pavilion was opened in 1928 and honours old boys killed in the Great War.

Bee Hive Inn

The original Bee Hive Inn — with its distinctive carved beehive sign — stood from *c.* 1770 on the western side of Lairgate, close to the Keldgate junction. However, the dram shop window was a later addition, made in 1876 by Robert Stephenson (of the Golden Ball). Hull Breweries closed the pub in 1957 along with the nearby Tanners Arms in Keldgate. A new Beehive was built in Keldgate in 1958. However, it too has how been demolished and replaced by the modern Beehive House.

Lairgate, 1912

Lairgate was also badly affected by the flash flood of July 1912. In the distance is the Tiger, another eighteenth-century inn, originally known as the Black Bull. In the 1820s the inn had its own brewhouse but by 1912 it was serving ales from Darley's Thorne Brewery. It had been renamed following the closure of the Tiger Inn on North Bar Within in 1847 and was refurbished in 1931. Many of the cottages seen here have since been replaced by modern developments.

Lairgate, c. 1910

Hebb Brothers garage (left — with flagpole) was situated at Nos. 87-9 Lairgate. Like others in Beverley, the Hebbs seized the opportunities presented by new technology. In 1899 James (a labourer) and Francis (an agent for artificial manure) were living here. By 1905 they had started up as cycle agents and motor engineers, and in the 1920s they moved to Cross Street. The long wall (right) enclosed the extensive grounds of Lairgate Hall, the eighteenth-century home of the Pennyman family.

Lairgate, c. 1904

The wall (right) extended north beyond the modern Champney Road. The Memorial Hall (left) was built in 1840 as St John's Anglican chapel. It closed in 1939 but reopened twenty years later as a community hall named in honour of all Beverlonians who served during the Second World War. Beverley Corporation purchased Lairgate Hall in 1926, building Admiral Walker Road and developing the grounds for council housing. The hall itself was used by local government until reorganisation in 1996 and is now an office complex.

Keldgate, *c.* 1906

Fife and drums precede men of the East Yorkshire Regiment as they march into town. They too are passing the wall of Lairgate Hall — part of which still stands here today. The kitchen gardens (with hothouse) extended down to this corner. Once a popular residential street with several fine houses, including the Old Grammar School (*c.* 1696), Keldgate was until 1986 also home to a tannery. Run latterly by Melrose Tanners, part of the site is now a housing development, Melrose Park.

Keldgate Bar

Keldgate (or South) Bar existed *c.* 1250 (when Keldgate was known as Southbargate). Rebuilt in brick during the fifteenth century, it was demolished in 1808. To either side lay the town ditch — to the south much used for tannery effluent in the nineteenth century, to the west now the site of the Leases. The single-storey cottages adjoining the bar were replaced in 1863 by the Elizabeth Westowby almshouse, built to accommodate three poor persons.

Victoria Barracks, Queensgate, *c.* 1906

As the county town, close links with the military feature strongly in Beverley's past — through the East Riding Militia and the East Yorkshire Regiment. In the 1870s army reforms placed great emphasis on local recruitment. The East Yorkshires consequently needed a permanent Beverley base and a barracks was built in 1877. Subsequent reorganisations made it redundant and it closed in 1961. Morrisons eventually bought the site and opened there in 1992, in a building designed to recall the old barracks.

The Old Fire Station, Albert Terrace, c. 1907

The Beverley (C) Company, 2nd Volunteer Battalion, East Yorkshire Regiment pose outside their HQ — since 1987 a health centre. First opened in 1861 as the Foundation or Middle Class School, the Grammar School briefly found a home here after it was refounded in 1890. When that school moved to Queensgate in 1902 the building became a drill hall. In 1950 it was taken over by East Riding Fire Brigade, remaining as Beverley's fire station until the move to New Walkergate in 1983.

Westwood, 1887

The 2nd Volunteer Battalion is in camp close to the Union Mill (or Anti-mill), once one of five mills on Westwood. Built in 1799 by the Union Mill Society, the mill operated as a cooperative, in competition with private owners accused of overcharging. The upper part of the tower was eventually dismantled, and in 1896 the base became (and remains part of) the clubhouse of Beverley and East Riding Golf Club.

Black Mill, Westwood, *c.* 1860

Formed in 1889, the Golf Club was previously based at the Black Mill. Cricket was also played here regularly between *c.* 1825 and 1909, when the Norwood Park recreation ground was opened. A mill has stood here since the 1650s, but the present structure (also known as Far, High or Baitson's Mill) was rebuilt by Gilbert Baitson in 1803 on a sixty-five-year lease. After damage by fire, its working gear was removed by the Pasture Masters when the lease expired in 1868.

Beverley Racecourse, 1903

The cup so prominently displayed here is the 1903 Watt Memorial Plate. The race was first held in 1885 and was won on this occasion by Mr Reid's Cliftonhall. Organised races have been held on Westwood and Hurn for over 300 years. Stands followed somewhat later — the first in 1767 and a second (seen here) in 1887. Both were demolished in 1928. Racing remains popular in Beverley, with twenty race days scheduled for 2010 and many improvements to the course in recent years.

Willow Grove, 24 July 1912 and 25 June 2007

In 1912 a cloudburst saw nearly two inches of rainfall in ninety minutes, and the old riverbed in Newbald Road became a 'raging torrent', collecting in the low ground at the end of Willow Grove. The summer of 2007 was the wettest since then. On 25 June one sixth of the area's annual rainfall was recorded in less than twelve hours. Houses in Willow Grove were among those flooded and the land before them once again became a lake.

East Riding Sessions House
Built 1805-10, the Sessions House incorporated a court with a prison to the rear. By 1835 the prison had 126 cells, but forty years later its inmate population averaged only half that number. Inside, the courtroom retained many of its original features and fittings until its closure in 2002 with the opening of the new Magistrates Court. The main building has now been converted into a health spa, the southern wing accommodates a restaurant and the northern wing Beverley Police Station.

New Walk, *c.* 1870

New Walk was first laid out by Beverley Corporation in the 1780s as a shady promenade for ladies and gentlemen. The regular lines of chestnut trees replaced more varied and irregular plantings in 1822, while most of the houses are late Victorian. For some years, New Walk has provided a picturesque finish for the East Yorkshire Classic road race, won in July 2009 by Dutchman Wouter Sybrandy. The white house (farthest right) is visible in the distance of the nineteenth-century image.

North Bar, July 1910
Passers-by cluster outside the gates of North Bar, closed for three days on 23 July 1910 so the road could be repaired.

Acknowledgements

Pat Deans has built up her collection over a long period and wishes to acknowledge her debt to all those who, over the years, have given copies of illustrations from their own collections. In the absence of a catalogue with details of provenance, it is impossible to thank by name all those who have contributed to this book, but the gratitude of the author is nonetheless sincere.

Margaret Sumner wishes to thank her husband, Ian, for all his help in photographing Beverley in 2009 and in researching the captions. She also wishes to acknowledge the work of the many authors — published and unpublished — who have done so much to expand our knowledge and understanding of the town.